M000103495

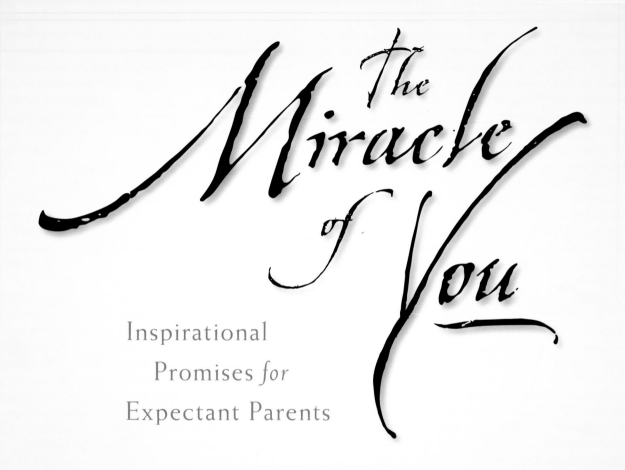

The Miracle of You

Inspirational
Promises *for*
Expectant Parents

KAREN WELLS *&* Illustrated by HEIDI FARNER

Kregel
Publications

The Miracle of You: Inspirational Promises for Expectant Parents

© 2009 by Karen Wells; illustrated by Heidi Farner

Published by Kregel Publications, a division of Kregel, Inc., P.O. Box 2607, Grand Rapids, MI 49501.

All rights reserved. No part of this book may be reproduced, stored in a retrieval system, or transmitted in any form or by any means—electronic, mechanical, photocopy, recording, or otherwise—without written permission of the publisher, except for brief quotations in printed reviews.

Scripture contained herein is the author's own paraphrase unless otherwise noted. While remaining true to the version indicated, some passages have been slightly modified to accommodate narrative flow and application.

Scripture quotations marked AMP are from the Amplified Bible, Copyright © 1954, 1958, 1962, 1964, 1965, 1987 by The Lockman Foundation. Used by permission. (www.Lockman.org)

Scripture quotations marked MSG are from *The Message*. Copyright © 1993, 1994, 1995, 1996, 2000, 2001, 2002. Used by permission of NavPress Publishing Group. All rights reserved.

Scripture quotations marked NIV are from the *Holy Bible, New International Version*®. Copyright © 1973, 1978, 1984 by International Bible Society. Used by permission of Zondervan. All rights reserved.

Scripture quotations marked NKJV are from the New King James Version. Copyright © 1982 by Thomas Nelson, Inc. Used by permission. All rights reserved.

Scripture quotations marked NLT are from the Holy Bible, New Living Translation, copyright © 1996, 2004. Used by permission of Tyndale House Publishers, Inc., Wheaton, Illinois 60189. All rights reserved.

ISBN 978-0-8254-3933-9

Printed in China

09 10 11 12 13 / 5 4 3 2 1

Heidi and I would like to dedicate this book
to our beautiful children . . .
Caleb, Naomi, and KariAnna
Wesley, Joshua, and Rachel
1 Chronicles 17:16–27

And in loving memory of my father . . .
Kent Nuckols
Dad began this project with me as the original illustrator.
Though he never saw it to completion in his hands, he saw
it in his heart. I want to thank him for believing in me.
Because of him, I know I can do all things
through Christ who strengthens me.

ongratulations! Children are truly a miraculous gift from above. How exciting to be entrusted with such a precious gift!

Now begins one of the most exciting times of your life. This season promises to be one of new beginnings and hope for the future. Undeniably with every new chapter of life, excitement is always coupled with things unknown. And to prepare for the unknown, you will undoubtedly buy, or be given, books containing helpful pregnancy information and advice.

This book, however, is not your typical pregnancy resource. In essence, it is a "prenatal children's book," meant to be read to your baby before he or she is even born! Studies show that by the time of birth, babies may be able to recognize the familiar sounds of fifty to one hundred words. Reading this book to your baby is a wonderful way to increase bonding and stimulate brain function. The true power, though, lies in *what* you are speaking to your baby.

Inspired by Scripture, the text on each page correlates to pivotal anatomical, psychological, and spiritual milestones of your baby's development. These passages were chosen because they represent God's heartbeat toward this new, forming life and prove His passion and plans for the "littlest ones." The words you speak are not just idle words. They are spirit and life; full of living power.

In addition to growing your faith in God's purposes for your baby, my hope is to equip you with a powerful tool in godly parenting and to help you lay a solid foundation of praying for your children from before they are even born! The most effective prayers I have prayed for my children are the ones that come straight from God's Word.

As you read, believe with all your heart that you will see the fulfillment of all the promises God has for you and your little one—during your pregnancy, throughout labor and delivery, in the first days, and for the rest of his or her life.

Blessings to you and your baby!

Karen

"The words I have spoken to you are spirit and they are life." —*John 6:63 NIV*

"For the word of God is full of living power." —*Hebrews 4:12*

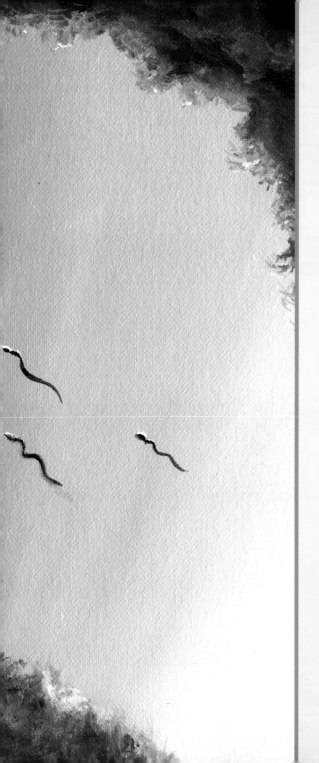

God saw you before you were born. Every day of your life was recorded in His book. Every moment was laid out before a single day had passed.

—*Psalm 139:16 NLT*

The Lord's message to you is, "I knew you before I formed you in your mother's womb. Before you were born I set you apart and appointed you as my spokesperson to the world."

—*Jeremiah 1:5 NLT*

WEEKS 1 & 2

Before conception, Mother's body is preparing a place for Baby.

You are wanted, loved, and will be dedicated to God's purposes every day of your life.

—*1 Samuel 1:27–28*

God created you in His very own image. He patterned you after Himself. Whether you are boy or girl, God is your creator.

—*Genesis 1:27*

WEEKS 3 & 4

The little one's journey begins now with precise, intricate multiplication and rapid growth.

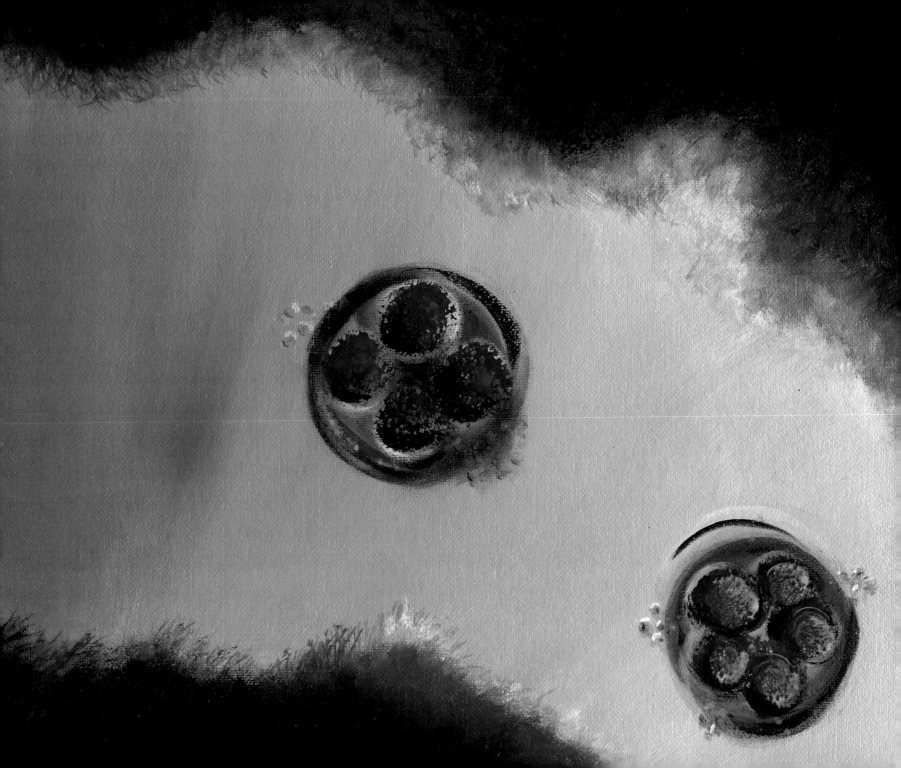

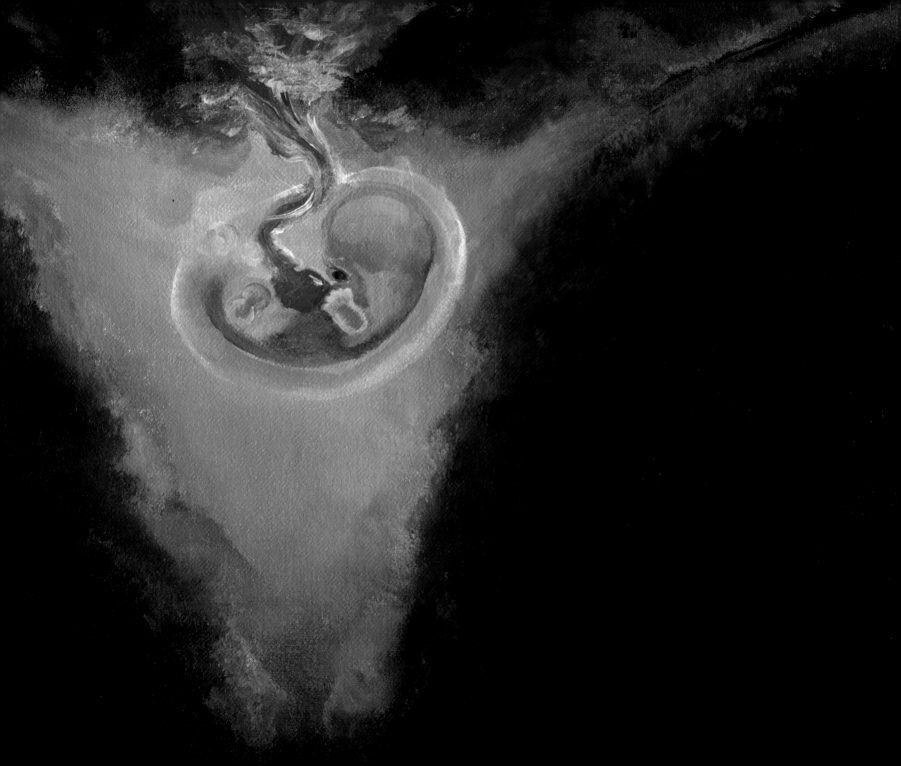

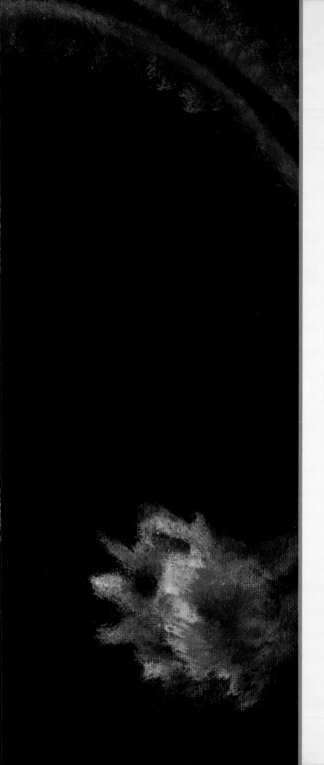

God watches as you are formed in utter seclusion, as He weaves you together in the dark of the womb.

—Psalm 139:15 NLT

Your heart is firmly fixed, trusting in the Lord. Your heart is established and steady.

—Psalm 112:7–8 AMP

WEEKS 5 & 6

The precious heart, no bigger than a poppy seed, has begun to beat.

God arranges the parts in your body, every one of them, just as He wants them to be.

—*1 Corinthians 12:18 NIV*

God spreads His protection over you . . . He surrounds you with His shield of love.

—*Psalm 5:11–12 NLT*

WEEKS 7 & 8

Baby's kidneys, lungs, and nerves take shape, and she can move her arms and legs underneath the safe covering of the amniotic sac.

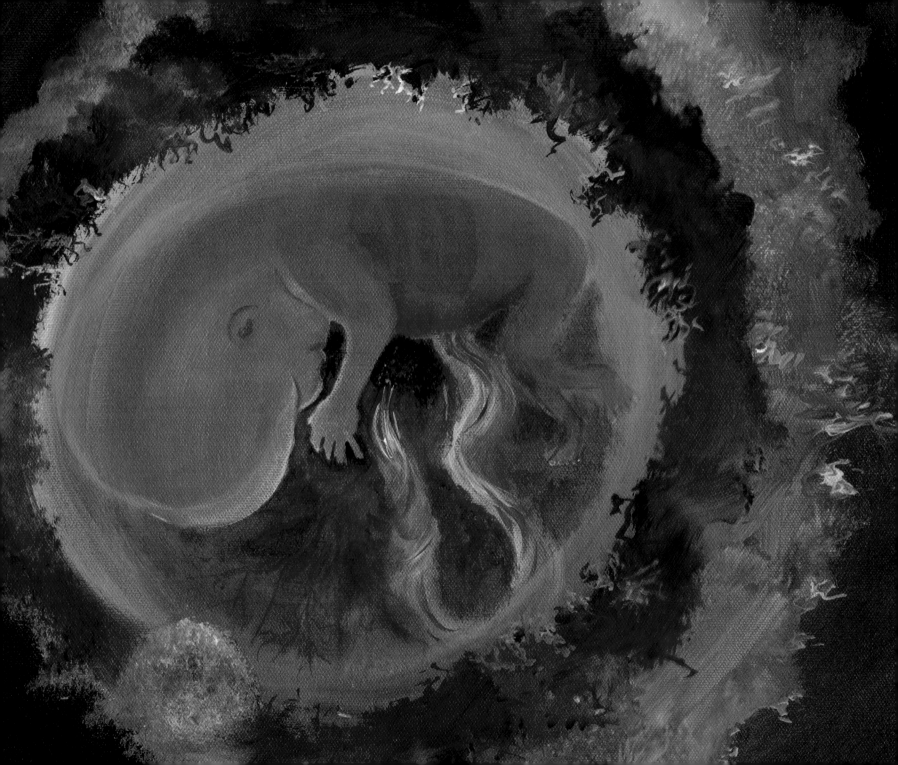

God is your shelter. You dwell in the secret place of the Most High and you will remain stable and fixed under the shadow of the Almighty.

—Psalm 91:1 AMP

You are God's best gift; the fruit of your mother's womb, a generous legacy.

—Psalm 127:3 MSG

WEEKS 9 & 10

The major organs begin to function as Baby burrows deeper into the shelter of the womb.

Your body will glow with health, your very bones will vibrate with life!

—*Proverbs* 3:8 *MSG*

Your body will be a temple of the Holy Spirit. . . . You are not your own; you were bought at a price. Therefore honor God with your body.

—*1 Corinthians* 6:19–20 *NIV*

WEEKS 11 & 12

Around two inches long, Baby's body takes full shape from the head to the hardening bones in the tiny toes.

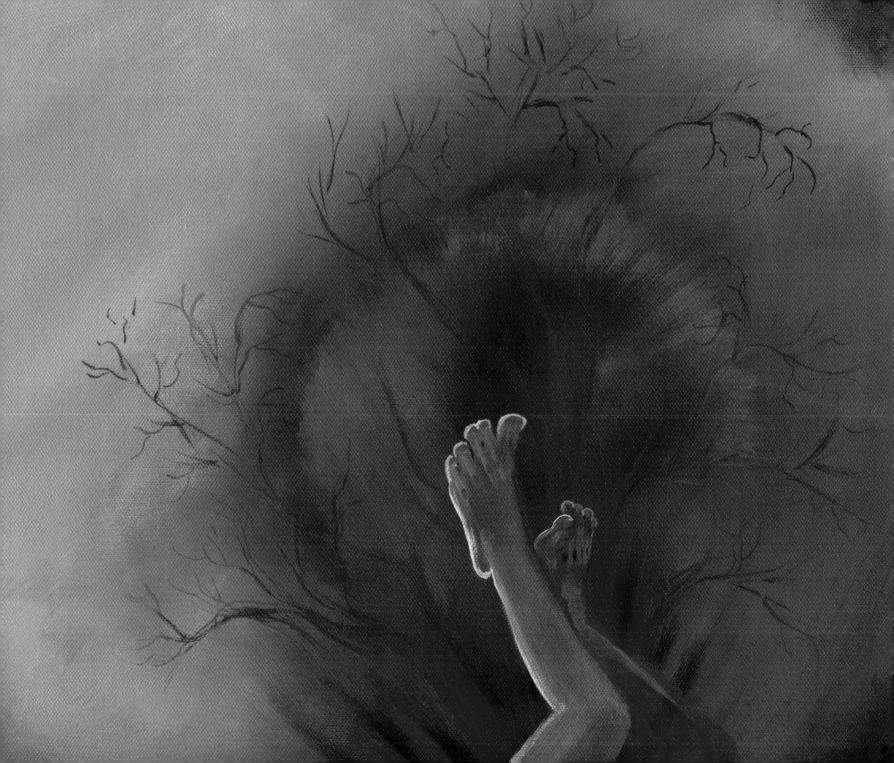

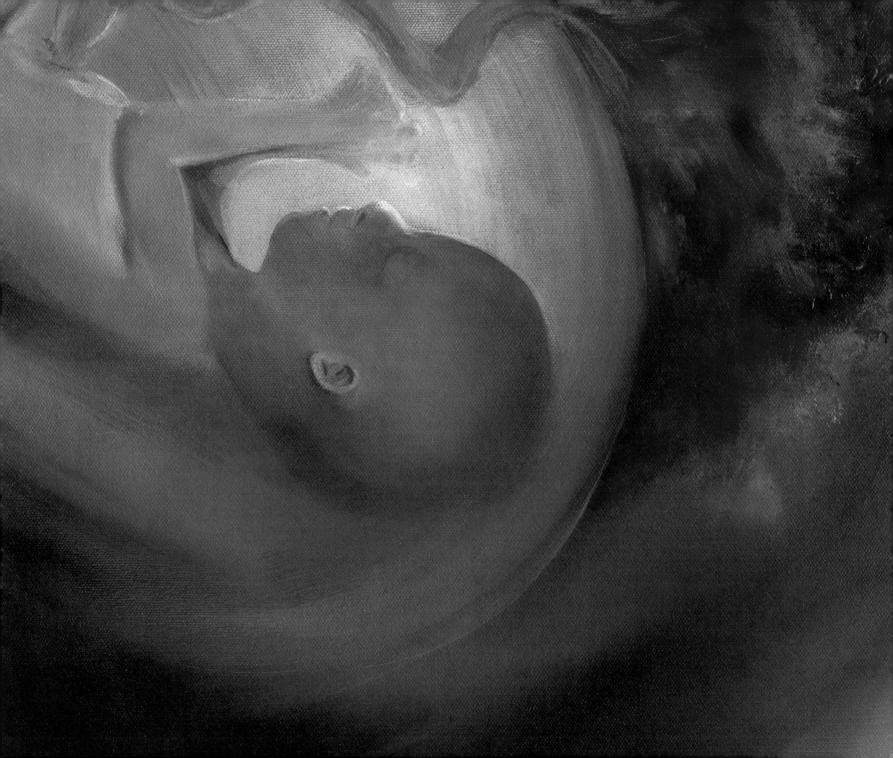

Tune your ears to the voice of the Lord . . . as you discover His words, you will live, really live; body and soul, you are bursting with health.

—*Proverbs* 4:20–22 MSG

You are devoted to God and you recognize His voice. He knows you as a shepherd knows his sheep and you follow Him. He gives you eternal life, and you will never perish. No one can snatch you away from Him.

—*John* 10:27–28

WEEKS 13 & 14

Baby's ears form so wonderfully, he can begin to sense outside sounds and voices.

God pays great attention to you, down to the last detail. . . .
Every detail of your body and soul—even the hairs of your
head!—is in His care; nothing of you will be lost.

—Matthew 10:30 and Luke 21:18 MSG

God will free you from all your fears. As you look to Him for
help, you will be radiant with joy.

—Psalm 34:4–5 NLT

WEEKS 15 & 16

A very fine hair, called lanugo, forms all over Baby's body.
She has little eyebrows and eyelashes.

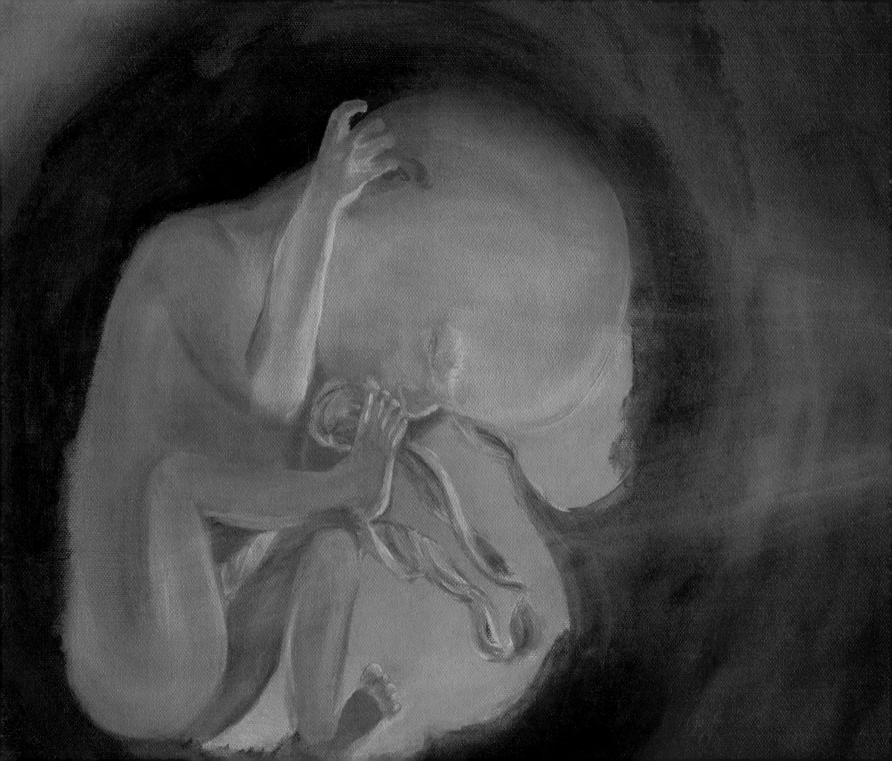

God, Himself, has magnificently designed you, and with the great delicacy of a master craftsman, He is shaping you inside the womb.

—*Psalm 139:13*

God will pour His Spirit on you, and you will thrive wherever He plants you.

—*Isaiah 44:3–4*

WEEKS 17 & 18

Baby's movements are getting stronger. Mom will begin to be more aware of his "quickening" presence.

You belong to God; He holds your right hand. He guides you with counsel, leading you to a glorious destiny.

—*Psalm 73:23–24 NLT*

Even before you are born, God is choosing you and calling you by His marvelous grace.

—*Galatians 1:15 NLT*

WEEKS 19 & 20

The five senses become more refined. Swirl patterns on the fingertips begin to map out Baby's unique fingerprints.

How sweet are His words to your taste, sweeter than honey to your mouth! . . . His word is a lamp to your feet and a light for your path.

—Psalm 119:103, 105 NIV

There is not the slightest doubt in my mind that the God who started this great work in you will keep at it and bring it to a flourishing finish.

—Philippians 1:6 MSG

WEEKS 21 & 22

Halfway through pregnancy, taste buds develop on Baby's tongue, and her digestive system is absorbing water from the amniotic fluid she swallows.

The same God who takes care of me will supply all your needs from His glorious riches, which have been given to us in Christ Jesus.

—Philippians 4:19 NLT

Overwhelming victory is yours through Christ, who loves you. Be convinced that nothing can ever separate you from God's love.

—Romans 8:37–38 NLT

WEEKS 23 & 24

The umbilical cord connects Baby to the placenta. This organ supplies vital nourishment and support.

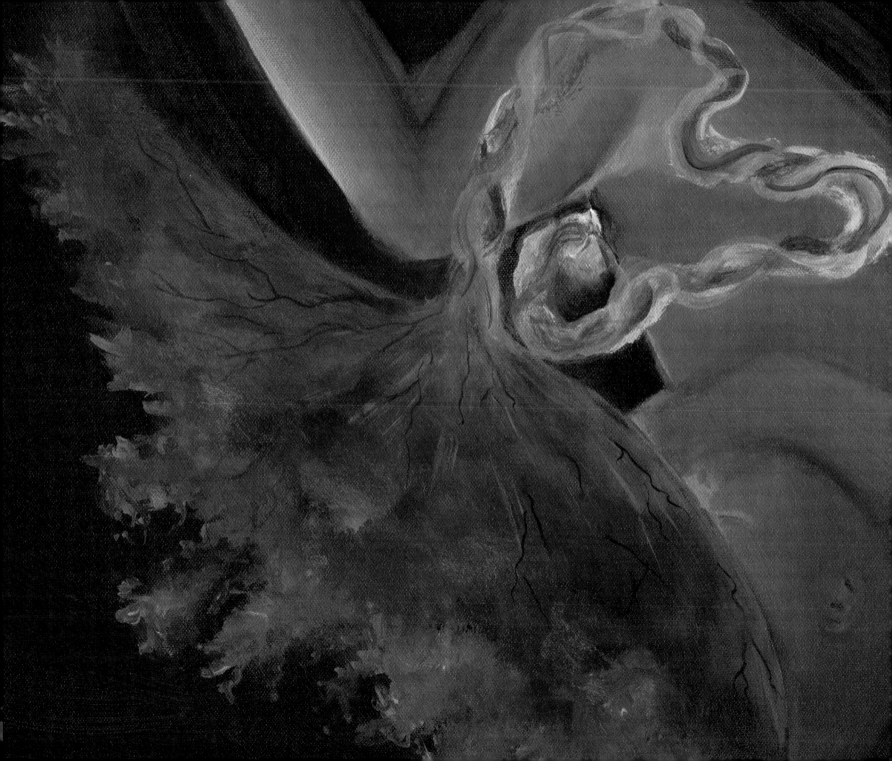

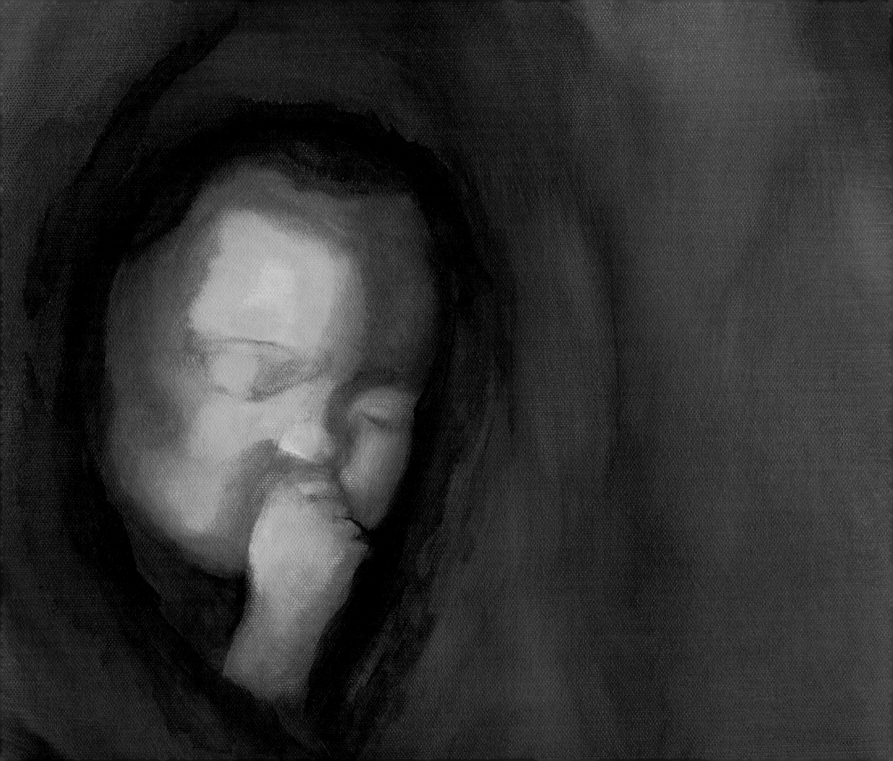

You'll take afternoon naps without a worry, you'll enjoy a good night's sleep. . . . Because God will be right there with you; He'll keep you safe and sound.

—*Proverbs* 3:24, 26 *MSG*

As God leads and guides you, you will be at peace. Your foundation is built on righteousness, and no enemy can come against you.

—*Isaiah* 54:13–14

WEEKS 25 & 26

Baby cycles through patterns of wakefulness and sleep. Though he is taking naps most of the day, his activities may include holding his feet, sucking his thumb, or playing with his cord.

God has made this light shine in your heart so you can know
the glory of God that is seen in the face of Jesus Christ.

—*2 Corinthians 4:6 NLT*

Be strong and empowered by faith as you give praise and glory
to God, fully satisfied and assured that God is able and mighty
to keep His word and to do what He has promised.

—*Romans 4:20–21 AMP*

WEEKS 27 & 28

*Opening and shutting her eyes, Baby becomes more aware of the
outside world; she even senses patches of light and darkness.*

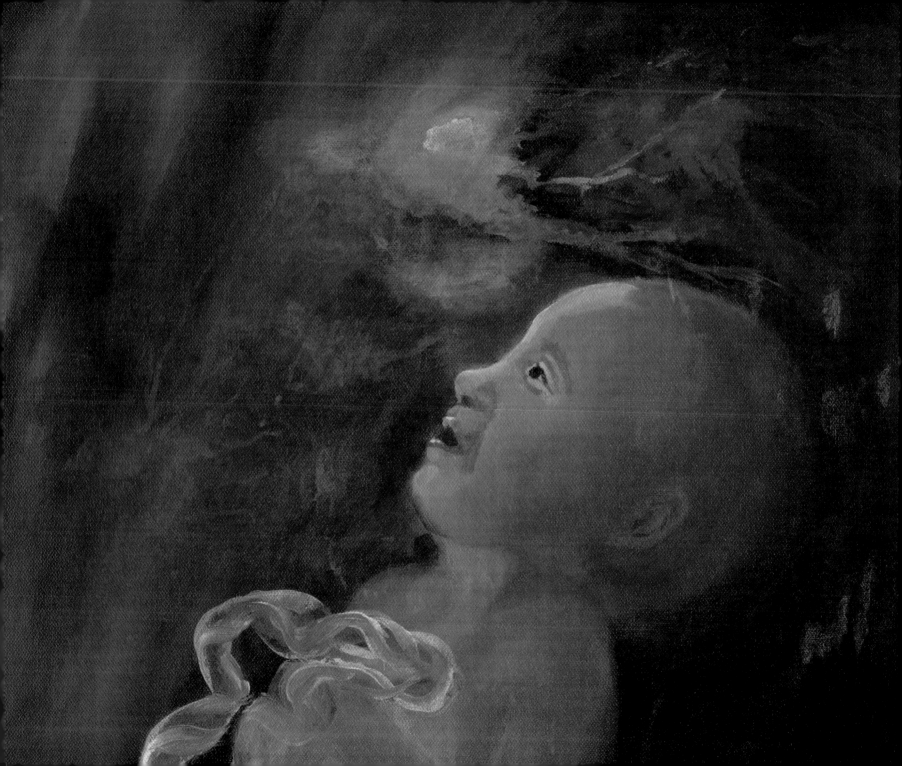

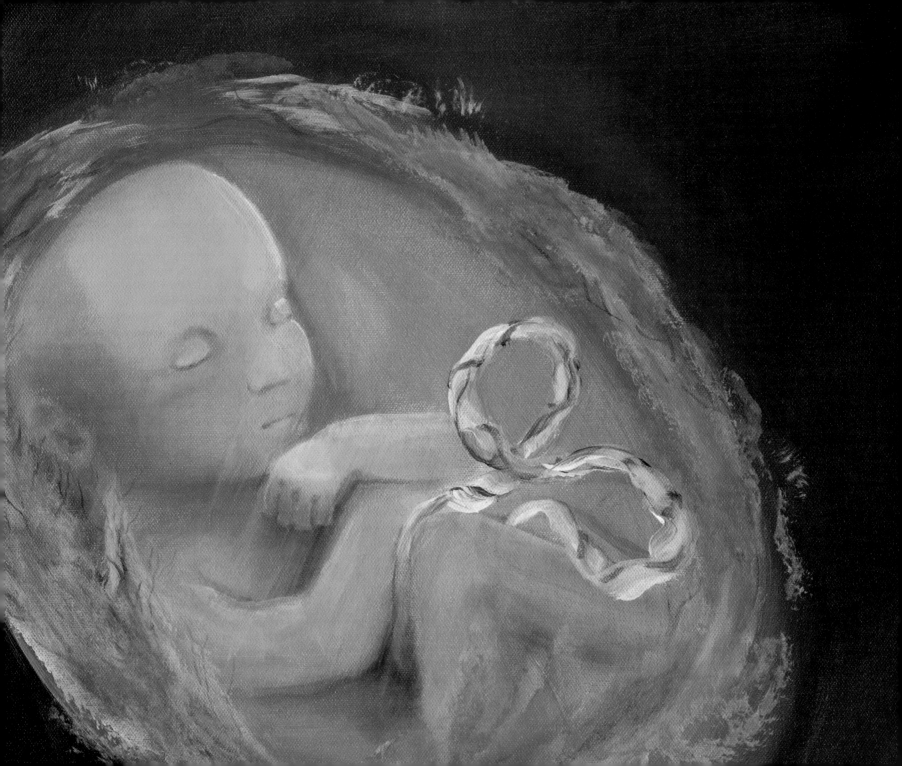

You will say of the Lord, "He is my Refuge and my Fortress."
. . . God will cover you with His feathers. He will shelter you
with His wings. His faithful promises are your armor and
protection.

—Psalm 91:2 AMP and 91:4 NLT

God has not given you a spirit of fear, but of power and of love
and of a sound mind.

—2 Timothy 1:7 NKJV

WEEKS 29 & 30

*Gaining in size and power, the brain quickly grows and builds strong
neurological connections. Baby's muscle movements are more refined
even though his available space is decreasing.*

You are in a place of worship, drinking in His strength and glory. In His generous love, you are really living!

—*Psalm 63:2–3 MSG*

Your lips brim praises like fountains. You bless God every time you take a breath; your arms wave like banners of praise.

—*Psalm 63:3–4 MSG*

WEEKS 31 & 32

With a careful eye, Mom might be able to watch Baby practice her breathing—inhaling and exhaling fluid, strengthening the lungs.

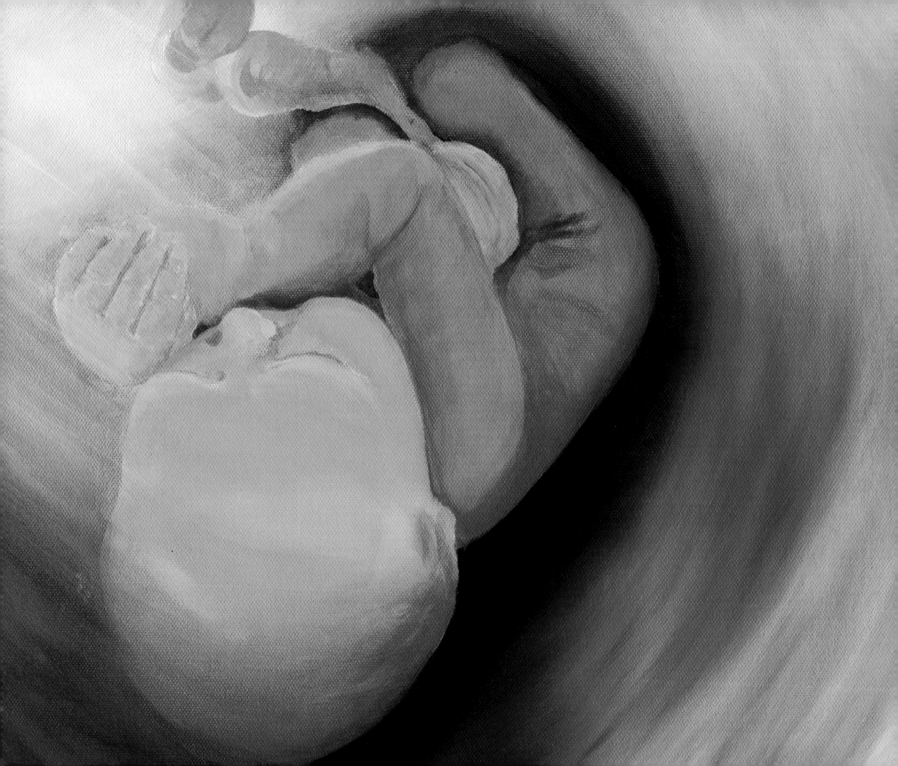

God will give His angels charge over you to accompany and
defend and preserve you in all your ways of obedience and
service. . . . He will satisfy you with long life and show you His
salvation.

—*Psalm 91:11, 16 AMP*

Wisdom will enter your heart, and knowledge will fill you with
joy. Wise choices will watch over you. Understanding will
keep you safe.

—*Proverbs 2:10–11 NLT*

WEEKS 33 & 34

*Looking more like a newborn, Baby begins early learning by
interacting with Mom as she taps on her belly, and by recognizing
familiar sounds and voices.*

God will guard you and keep you in perfect and constant
peace. . . . So trust in the Lord—commit yourself to Him, lean
on Him, hope confidently in Him—forever; for the Lord God
is your everlasting Rock.

—Isaiah 26:3–4 AMP

Let no one despise your youth, but be an example to the
believers in word, in conduct, in love, in spirit, in faith, in
purity.

—1 Timothy 4:12 NKJV

WEEKS 35 & 36

*Already around five or six pounds, most of the development is
complete. Baby will continue growth by gaining weight and filling out
the wrinkles and folds in his skin.*

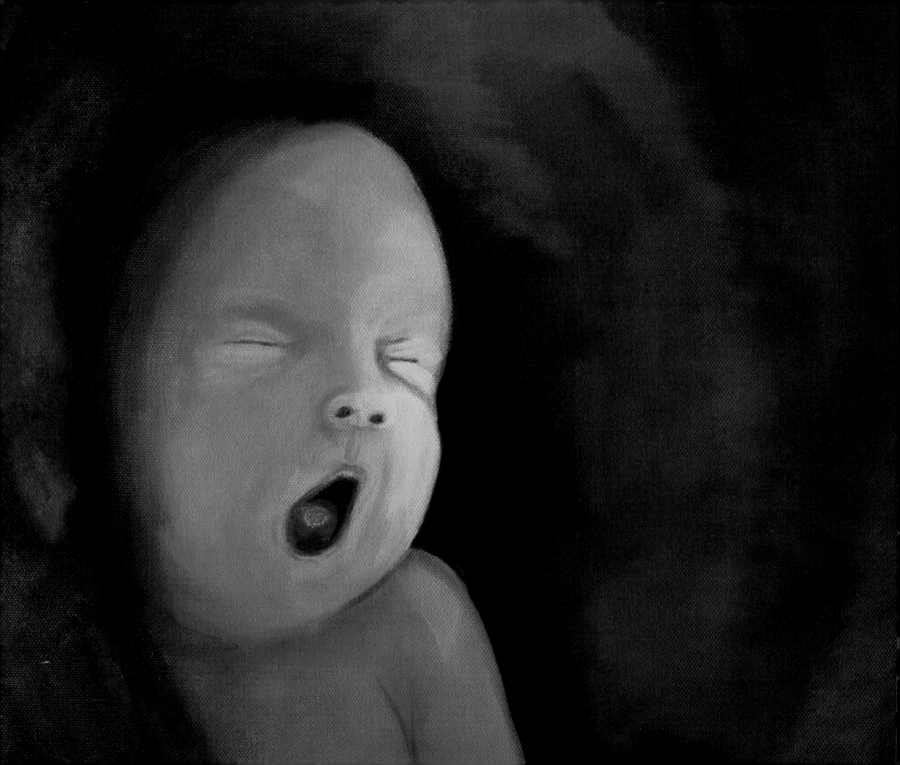

Out of the mouths of babies and infants, God has made perfect praise.

—*Matthew 21:16 AMP*

You are not too young for God to use you. You will go where He tells you to go and say what He tells you to say without fear, because He will be with you all the way.

—*Jeremiah 1:7–8*

WEEKS 37 & 38

Baby's lungs, central nervous system, and digestive tract are in the final stages of maturing, almost ready for life outside the womb.

The Lord will watch over your coming and going both now
and forevermore.

—*Psalm 121:8 NIV*

You can do everything through Christ who gives you strength.
. . . For nothing is impossible with God.

—*Philippians 4:13 and Luke 1:37 NIV*

WEEKS 39 & 40

Well worth the wait, Baby's grand entrance is almost here!

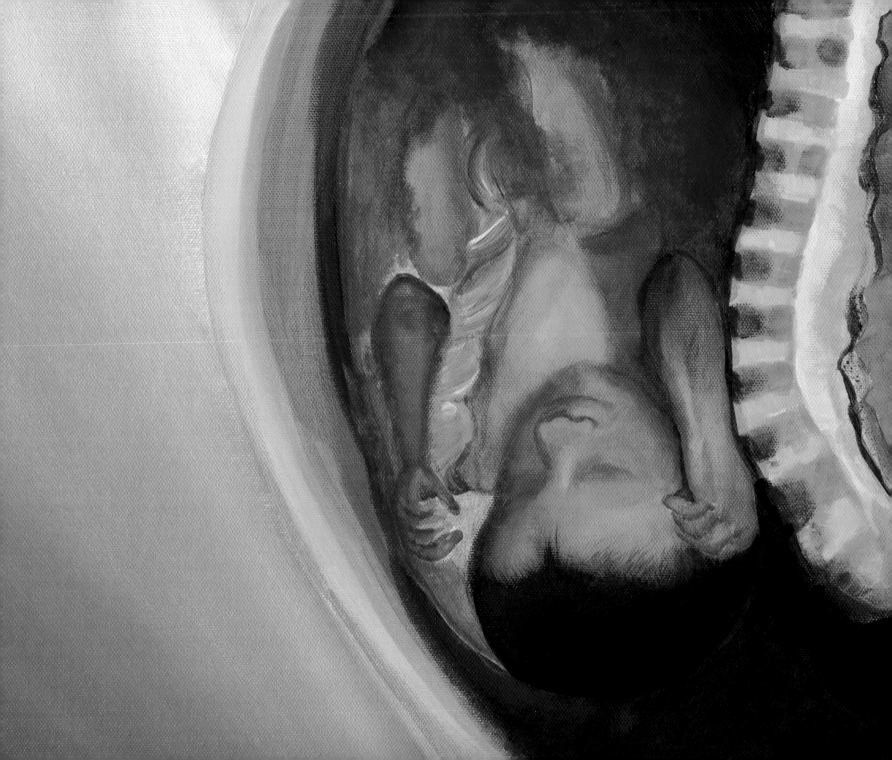

"For I know the plans I have for you," declares the Lord, "plans to prosper you and not to harm you, plans to give you hope and a future."

—*Jeremiah* 29:11 *NIV*

God's plan is for you to be a joy and delight. Many will rejoice because of your birth. You will be great in His sight. You will turn many sons and daughters of God back to the Lord. You will have the spirit and power to turn the hearts of the fathers to their children. . . . And you, our little child, will be called of the Most High to prepare a way for the Lord. You will tell His people how to find salvation through the forgiveness of sins and with His tender mercy you will give light to those who sit in darkness and the shadow of death, guiding them to the path of peace.

—*Luke* 1:14—17, 76—79

Welcome to this world!